Photograph by Christopher Barker, probably Sutherland Place, London, date unknown.

'A PATCH OF EARTH':

John Heath-Stubbs's Hampshire Poems

'A PATCH OF EARTH':

John Heath-Stubbs's Hampshire Poems

Front: The earliest known photograph of John Heath-Stubbs

Back: 1875 wood engraving of the New Forest, artist unknown

ISBN: 9798267735018

Paul R. Secord Books
Albuquerque, New Mexico

TABLE of CONTENTS

INTRODUCTION

POEMS

INTRODUCTION

John Heath Stubbs, Hampshire's Blind Poet and His Amanuensis

by Adrian Risdon and Jack Wilson (June 20, 2022); from "In-Common - Southampton" <**www.in-common.co.uk**>

Jack: I recently wrote an article on *Bevis of Southampton*, which evoked a response that will be fascinating for all those with an interest in poetry and poets. I was contacted by Adrian Risdon, who explained that he was once amanuensis to the famous blind poet John Heath-Stubbs, amongst whose works was a poem named *Bevis of Hampton*.

Heath-Stubbs' first 21 years were largely spent in the New Forest at Barton and New Milton, and he attended Bembridge boarding-school on the Isle of Wight in his teens. Diagnosed with glaucoma in his childhood, he was completely blind from 1978. Nonetheless, he continued to write almost to the end, helped by Adrian and others.

Adrian: Despite two Cambridge degrees, my employment history proved a disaster. I couldn't cope as a schoolmaster, and after acting as warden for two Carr-Gomm hostels, eventually settled for clerical work in the Civil Service. Later, personal complications meant that Job Centres forced me into a long succession of increasingly pointless and poorly paid occupations, but my voluntary work was both more satisfying and much more successful, especially my time with John.

I first met John in 1976, as a consequence of a conversation on the top deck of a London bus with a disdainful nun. "Mr Heath-Stubbs," she snootily remarked, "dwells in total squalor." The combination of scholar and squalor I found immensely attractive. So I posted John a copy of my thesis on Dante, he invited me to read it to him – and things went on from there. For 30 years I assisted him in a variety of ways, joined the "Heath-Stubbs Circle," and attended his very literary parties.

John could be a difficult person to work with. When once I suggested it was O.K. for people to enjoy both his own verse **and** that of Philip Larkin (with whom he had had a falling-out), he snarled: "I think you'd better leave." Next morning he was on the phone to apologise; he'd had a dream in which he and Larkin were friends again, and had based a new poem on the dream.

 John was very conflicted in his feelings about the Hampshire he grew up in and (emotionally) never really left. Despite an international academic career, his mind regularly returned here – leading to such amazing 'local' poems as "Bevis of Hampton" and "Purkis" – the latter about the charcoal-burner who trundled William Rufus's corpse from the New Forest to Winchester – as well as "Old Mobb," the Romsey highwayman. He recites Purkis to my friend Colin and myself on a short film we made, "At Home with John Heath-Stubbs."

I sometimes think of John as being like the Bargate – an antique structure stubbornly surviving amidst much modern dross. He himself might wryly have identified with New Milton's Water Tower – another building with an air of being slightly out-of-place (and out-of-time). But a poem like "Bevis of Hampton" gives his potential readers hereabouts a real opportunity to take him and his poetry to their hearts. When I moved from Winchester to Southampton in 2001, John's response was surprising and encouraging: "Southampton is," he opined, "more of a real city."

Jack: Since John's death in 2006, Adrian has devoted a large portion of his time to promoting his (John's) poetry. He firmly believes John to be "the best Poet Laureate England never had." We intend to publish "Bevis of Hampton," with notes by Adrian, and then more about John, and particularly his Hampshire poetry.

Adrian is himself a published poet. His work includes a poem on a Gay Pride March in Southampton in 2017, from which the following lines are taken:

> *We march along Above Bar Street (or straggle)*
> *depending on this script's veracity) ...*
> *Over the distant Bargate, like an eagle,*
> *our Rainbow flag's flying defiantly –*
> *Ancient and Modern, gay and the superseded –*
> *where, thinks John's ghost, the Union Jack should be.*

Adrian Risdon is a Brother at the Hospital of St. Cross, Winchester.
Jack Wilson is a *See Southampton Tourist Guide.*

See: <https://www.youtube.com/watch?v=74LUdhF5cAA> for a video of Adrian Risdon discussing John Heath-Stubbs.

1.

CHURCHYARD OF SAINT MARY MAGDALENE, OLD MILTON

Here, where my father lies under the ornamental plum,
Geese step in the next farm-field, while to the Rectory elms
The rooks fly home. *Dominus exaltatio mea* -
The eagle rising with its sprig of acorns.

Feet deep in sticky clay, under the kempt grasses,
Under the Anglo-Saxon and the Celtic crosses,
The Indian judges lie, the admirals, the solicitors,
The eccentric ladies and the shopkeepers,
The unenterprising who would not go to the town,
The charwoman with a cleft palate, the jobbing gardener,
And the four Germans who fell, some few years back,
Out of a sky of trouble, smashed
In an empty field - these have
Their regulation crosses too, of wood,

And scattered flowers, left by the prisoners:
The old woman whom I meet
Remarks that after all they were somebody's sons
And we would do as much for our people.

The writer returns to the scene of his childhood -
Where he loitered and looked at the rooks and the geese and the turkeys,

Or sought for wild barley by the churchyard gate -
The caterpillar-grass
Whose insect heads climb slowly up your sleeve;
The rootless writer - filling his town lungs
With a gust of country air. A grey afternoon,
And in the sky, the promise of evening's rain.

Where people come to take the air and die,
Ending their lives here on an adequate pension,

A sickly child, brought there by careful parents,
Might mend in the salt breeze. From six to twenty-four
Home was this scattered residential village of bungalows,

Of gabled villas and neglected fallows,
Crazy paving, gravel and tarmac.
Now he comes back
And stands unrecognized among these graves.

The church here under John, that lackland king
(The guide-book says), rebuilt under Elizabeth:
(The tower still stands, four-square, looks down upon
The village green, a row of shops, a garage
Crimson and yellow with petrol-pumps,
A line of cottages, a blacksmith's forge -
A child, I remember that darkness and smoke and music -
Two adjacent public-houses, the George and Wheatsheaf,
And the post-office store, where stands behind the jumble
Of picture-postcards, cigarettes and buttons
The dusty case with its stuffed gannet and guillemot).
Rebuilt under Elizabeth, restored under Victoria
(The green distempered walls, peeling to white patches
Which took, at sermon-time, the shapes of islands -
White islands, in a green smooth-glistening sea).

Lie here the serfs, the yeomen and the gentry,
Under their mounds and single stones and vaults yellow with lichen;
Of all those faces, one only gazes still -
Queen Anne's colonel, in effigy, pompous his armour,
His helmet beside him, a ringleted wig of stone
Framing his vacant brow. His sword, that steel blade,
Which he drew against the French, is hung above him
Over the blurred inscription, on the left of the porch.

A torch borne in the wind, a drift of sparks and smoke
As the racer rounds the track in the bright sunlight,

Dust-puff, and dream, and shadow. . . .
A drop of rain, a large warm drop,
A rustle in the tresses of the elm,
A breath of perfume, twitched by the light breeze
From the fading flowers laid on the Italian marble -
But these evoke the sudden splendour of bright hair
Unloosed from the darkness of a penitent snood,
Sweetness and the splintering of the alabaster-sealed heart;
Somewhere among these tombs a woman's voice is sobbing;

Among these fragments grope the white and delicate hands
Of the Anointer of the Dead, who comes in the dark hour
Bringing her spices for the early dawn.

A fountain of lamentation above the firmament, a human
River of tears that knows all streets, alleys and dark courts,
And bears upon its little waves
Sticks and straws and draggled cigarette-ends,
The gutter's refuse and corruption, on
Past Roman causeways, through black hearts of cities.
A girl, mad as grief, trudging the hard roads;
A woman, with a few ripe ears, in a country of famine;
The august queen of the shrunken banks of Nile,
Who seeks the body of her murdered Lord;
A girl, sorry as sin, and broken as contrition.

Lady of Magdala's tower, and the dower of Bethany,
You who are called patron here, forgive
The little lives, partial and fugitive existences,
The gestures of love frozen in a pose of propriety,
And starved desire, with malice that lies on a turning bed;

Forgive the tyrannies of the hearthstone, and the small politics
Of the local interest, the lonely and the dull.
Ask pardon for the community without a heart, and the betrayal
Of the backward years and the uncomplaining dead.
Carry these lives, these parts of lives, these yellow leaves
Drifted in autumn from the tree of the world
On tides of intercession, down
To a sea thirsty with love, where the breakers lift
White triumphing hands - insatiable -
And the free gull tacks to the courteous southern stars
With arched and frost-pale pinion:
Oh, in Death's garden be
Prime witness of the only Resurrection.

2.

FOR THE NINE-HUNDREDTH ANNIVERSARY OF WINCHESTER CATHEDRAL

Fall, rain, fall
Impartial as the grace of God,

On just and unjust - for Alfred,
Making his grave with the anonymous poor;

For the Red King, unloved, abandoned
In the dark grove, struck by the glancing arrow.
For the cardinal - before his tomb, in restitution
The glittering image of Joan the phoenix.

Wind from the Solent, Atlantic wind,
Bring rain at Swithin's behest -

For Izaak, who fished beside still waters,
When Test and Itchen went straying through Beulah;

For Jane, who delineated the human condition
On a small square of ivory;

For unknown builders' stone polyphony
For the singing pillars of Samuel Sebastian,

For the amiable habitation - descend
The former and latter rains.

3.

PURKIS

The red king lay in the black grove:
The red blood dribbled on moss and beech-mast.

With reversed horseshoes, Tyrrel has gone
Across the ford, scuds on the tossing channel.

Call the birds to their dinner. 'Not I,' said the hoarse crow,
'Not I,' whistled the red kite
'Will peck from their sockets those glazing eyes

Who will give him to his grave? 'Not I,' said the beetle
'Will shift one gram of ground under his corpse,
Nor plant in his putrid flank my progeny.'

Robin, red robin, will you in charity
Strew red Will with the fallen leaves?

'I cover the bodies of Christian men:
He lies unhouseled in the wilderness,
The desolation that his father made'.

Purkis came by in his charcoal-cart:
'He should lie in Winchester. I will tug him there -
Canons and courtiers perhaps will tip me,
A shilling or two for the charcoal-burner!

Purkis trundled through the town gates -
And 'Coals!' he cried: 'Coals, coals, coals,
Coals, charcoal, dry sticks for the burning!'

4.

BEVIS OF HAMPTON

Bevis waded ashore through the surf
Of four-tided Solent. At his heels
The delicate island was glimpsed,
Unglimpsed, through the mist:
Victoria watches the yachts
Flit to and fro, decrees
Tea and biscuits in the library
For Mr Gladstone, invites
Mr Disraeli to stay for dinner.

Bevis - his bones were chalk and his flesh was clay,
The crest of his helm
Royal and Roman Winchester;
Arthur's table,
An amulet, hung on his brow.
Gorse and fern of the New Forest
The scrubby hair on his chest and groin.

As his feet touched the shingle and undercliff, coltsfoot
Rest-harrow, scabious and knapweed
Blossomed about them - the Dartford warbler,
Stonechat and sand-martin spluttered a welcome.
Ponies obsequiously trotted forward -
They would convoy him inland.

I am Bevis, he shouted. I am Beow the barley-man.
I have been killing dragons and things In the Middle East;
now I come home To claim my inheritance.

His mouth was Southampton Water, where ships of
Tarshish, All the big steamers, chugged in and out, their
holds Bursting with biscuits you nibble, and beefsteaks.
Out of that throat the hymns of Isaac Watts
Arose in salutation to God and to judgement.

Miss Austen observed his coming
From the corner of her eye; on his shoulder, the down of Selborne -
There a retiring cleric discriminated the songs

Of willow-wren, chiffchaff, wood-wren.

Bevis - his right hand rested on Pompey and the great guns;
His left hand gently fondled
The dusty, fairy pavilions of Bournemouth.
In frozen horror a landlady
Stared at the ceiling, a spreading stain -
The blood of Alec D'Urberville.

The corner of his left sleeve
Lightly brushed the blue-slipper clay
Of the Barton beds, where Eocene fossils
Attested a former sub-tropical climate;
And curled asleep, in his middle-class room, a boy
Surmised he might be a poet.

5.

THE GLOBAL VILLAGE (Homage to Charlotte M. Yonge)

'Write novels, and submit them for publication?
Well of course I must insist
I should read through everything you write -
Read it and, if necessary, censor
And re-write it all.' Dutifully
She accepted her father's conditions
And she did write novels and they were printed
And they were best-sellers too. 'As for the profits,
He had also insisted, 'Every penny of course
Must go to charity, to worthy causes.'
This also she agreed to. And so it continued:
After his death, the same control
Was exercised by Keble -
Keble the poet of the Oxford Movement -
He happened to be her parish priest.
Hampshire was the county she was born in;

She died there too. It is a patch of earth
I also know well. So l imagine her
Going about her village of Otterbourne,
Full of good works, kind -
Not condescending - to the poor;
Writing her stories for young girls,
With a sharp eye for the small human follies
(Dramas transacted on the croquet lawn)
As Jane had had before in that same county
(But Jane's eye was clearer, her brushstrokes firmer,
Upon that little square of ivory).

Miss Yonge is walking beside a hawthorn hedgerow.
She stops to hear the whitethroat singing
Out of a nettlebed, and notices The musk-mallow, that
showy weed -
A Hampshire flower, a rarity elsewhere.

The phrase 'the global village'
Had not been coined in Charlotte's day.

But a trim ship, fitted and kitted out From royalties
The Heir of Redclyffe earned,
Was scudding amongst the South Pacific Islands
With a crew of Jolly Jacks and a complement
Of sober-suited clergymen, all filled
With post-Tractarian zeal to convert
Those lands where only Man is vile, and in the hold
A cargo of Bibles, books of Common Prayer,
Hymns translated by John Mason Neale
From Greek and Syriac, holy harmoniums,
Hassocks and cassocks, chasubles and albs.

Scent of exotic blossoms
Wafted on the balmy air. The palm-trees
Tossed their heads like the plumed heads of dancers.
The surf thundered upon the outer reef,
Gaudy with coral, where lurked
Scarlet-banded, deadly snakes, and fishes
Prickly and poison-bloated. A frigatebird,
Long-winged, piratical, bright pelican-pouches
Beneath its formidable beak,

Tail-forked, like an enormous swallow,
Was poised in the intense

Blue of a tropical sky. God's ebony children,
Hook-nosed and frizzy-haired, the Melanesians,
Flocked to the strange gospel. The fields
Were white for harvest.

Baptized, they still continued
To cultivate their yams, to collect
Their coconuts and pineapples, and feed
Their grunting droves of pigs. But Long Pig now
Was banished from their menus.
They'd exchanged Cannibalism for early fasting Eucharist;
Terror of ghosts and witchcraft
For sexual guilt, uncomfortable
Unnecessary clothes; subservience
To arbitrary, paranoiac chieftains
For new white masters, giving some protection
Against marauding blackbirders, perhaps.

Miss Yonge was ageing now, pottered along
Her village street, and marked
How housemartins were still collecting mud
From puddles in the road, to build their nests
Under the gutterings of that church
She had collected funds for; and later on
Pears would be ripening on a southward wall.
I think the village children liked her - had she not taught them
Their ABC, their catechism, and some
Of Mrs Alexander's hymns? Christ's promises
Are for all. But in her novels
It might be someone who purports to be
A philanthropic lecturer from Bristol
Who turns out really unreliable.

6.

HOUSEHOLD NOTES (1)

Emily it was, in Haworth parsonage,
Who made the bread. If you have kneaded dough
You'll know that you have got a living thing
Under your hands - and it fights back, fights back.
So, with firm fingers,
She squeezed the tumid viscous lumpish mass, Infusing in
it such suppressed emotions, And so much pent-up rage,
until she pushed it Into the oven. Resurrected
As bread, it was, I fancy, no less wholesome
For all that passion consubstantial with it.

HOUSEHOLD NOTES (2)

A few years back, and southward,
In another parsonage, Cassandra Austen
Used to make mead, a good Hampshire tradition.
Real mead, you know, isn't a sweet drink -
The honey-sugar turns to alcohol.
With a little mace, and zest of lemon-rind,
It's sharp and lucid - rather like, I'd say,
A dry white wine: but it is wholly English.
On suitable occasions
Her sister offered it to visitors -
Or was it ordinary, just for the servants?
Behind the converse was a murmuration -
The ghosts of bees, in their straw skeps,
Annihilated at the summer's end
With Sulphur, or with derris powder.

7.

OLD MOBB

Old Mobb stood on the Romsey Road:
A splendid equipage came along -
Inside was the Duchess of Portsmouth, with two French footmen,
And two sleek and pampered spaniels.
'Fellow,' she said, 'do you know who I am?'
'Yes, and what you are -
You are the king's whore, I think,
And not kind Protestant Nellie, neither!'
'Villain, do you dare to touch me there?'
'Now I command where the king asks his favours.'
Said Old Mobb, politely removing
Three hundred pounds, a little gold watch,
And a very splendid string of pearls.

Old Mobb was on the road at midnight:
Mercury, patron of thieves, swung in its orbit.
Came ambling by on an old grey mare

Mr John Gadbury the astrologer.
I am a poor man, a poor scholar,
Pray you, spare me!' 'What you -
Who lease out the seven stars for hire
To cozen noodles? These golden chimers
And these silver chinkers make better music
Than all the circling spheres, and much more audible,'
Said Old Mobb, as he pocketed them.
'You cannot rob me of my skill,' said Gadbury:
'In physiognomy and from your favour
I read you born for hanging.'

Came trotting along on a neat black pony
Dr Cornelius Tilburgh,
Successful physician with a bedside manner:
'Have you no care,' said he, 'for those
Your depredations ruined?'
'You, with your clysters and blisters, your nostrums and boluses,
Ruin more men than the cataracts of Nile.
Here, doctor, is a leaden pill -
Cough up, or void your superfluity:

No antidote, you know, for gunpowder!'
Said Old Mobb, as he extracted
Twenty-five pounds and a bright medal
With the king's own face upon it.

A proud coach rumbled along
On the road towards the Winchester Assizes.
Judge Jeffreys stuck his head out of the window -
His great full wig, his brazen blotchy face:
'The law has claws and I incorporate the law.
Don't think, my man, that you'll escape from justice.'
'Though I shall dance on Tyburn, and you
 Rot in the Tower, awaiting trial -
Yet there's another Judge we both must go to.
Who will fare better at those final sessions -
The Lord Chief Justice of England, he who hanged
Many poor men of the West at their own doorposts,
And doomed Dame Alice for her mere compassion
To broken fugitives - or a plain man of Hampshire
Who knew no master but his poverty?
Though he brandished a gun he never killed any

And prayed often
For God's forgiveness, even while he robbed;
As now I do,' said Old Mobb
Suiting the prigging action to the word.

8.

SQUIRLING

When the red nutkin (the rufous shadow-tail,
And not the grey American immigrant)
Danced in the branches of the lady-larch, or scolded
Down from the beech-tree boughs - this was,
By tradition, a Hampshire sport.

Two weights joined by a leather strap,
Sharply hurled, could bring the squirrel down.

'Barbarous?' the enquirer asked. 'Well,' said the old forester,
'At least we do eat the squirrel
Which is more than the gentry does the fox.'

9.

THE HEART'S FOREST

Since I am free, why do l linger here
   Among the shadows, while the impersonal train
   Stands ready to carry me from my despair,
   Shifting the mind's landscape with change-of-scene,

To that south country where the solitude
   Of field and forest can bring back again
   Only the sufferings of childhood
   When I was least troubled when most alone.

There, undisturbed by symbols, I may watch
   Successive flowers, at April's end to catch
   The first notes of the tentative nightingale;

But yet I could not bear that this sharp love
   Should seem unreal; you, central now to life,
   Fade from the heart, because incredible.

10.

OBSTINATE IN NON-ATTENDANCE

Obstinate in non-attendance I cannot but think kindly
Of the county of Hampshire, my nurse; she is sluttish but
not uncomely:
Sociable in London my heart is a parched forest
And my skull a stone tower where the songs not easily
nest.

But she who fostered my first cares and my loneliness,
Indifferent yet received them with a certain homeliness:
My tears hardly augment the griefs that in Thames must run,
But could add a saltness to the Stour's, or the Avon's, urn.

The Celt rants in my blood; but it is of Winchester
The Saxon monarchs who lift up a golden sceptre
To rule in all my dreams with a plain civility,
Though my ancestors rowed Edgar the Peaceable on the
Dee.

Or striving in my verse to acclimatise the Italian myrtle
And the Greek cyclamen, I sometimes feel it is futile:
The yellow gorse the coltsfoot and the rest-harrow
Are nourished by the clay and sand that fed my earliest sorrow.

CITY OF WESTMINSTER

JOHN
HEATH-STUBBS
O.B.E.
1918-2006

POET

LIVED HERE

FRIENDS OF JOHN HEATH-STUBBS

Printed in Dunstable, United Kingdom

70246818R00023